FREE-MOTION
meandering
A Beginner's Guide to Machine Quilting

ANGELA WALTERS

stashBOOKS.
an imprint of C&T Publishing

Text copyright © 2017 by Angela Walters

Photography and artwork copyright © 2017 by C&T Publishing, Inc.

Publisher: Amy Marson

Creative Director: Gailen Runge

Editor: Liz Aneloski

Technical Editor: Linda Johnson

Cover/Book Designer: April Mostek

Production Coordinators: Joe Edge and Zinnia Heinzmann

Production Editors: Jeanie German and Alice Mace Nakanishi

Illustrator: Aliza Shalit

Photo Assistant: Mai Yong Vang

Hand Model: Kristi Visser

Style photography by Lucy Glover and *Instructional photography by* Diane Pedersen of C&T Publishing, Inc., unless otherwise noted

Published by C&T Publishing, Inc., P.O. Box 1456, Lafayette, CA 94549

Library of Congress Cataloging-in-Publication Data

Names: Walters, Angela, 1979- author.

Title: Free-motion meandering : a beginner's guide to machine quilting / Angela Walters.

Description: Lafayette, California : C&T Publishing, Inc., [2017]

Identifiers: LCCN 2017006148 | ISBN 9781617455209 (soft cover)

Subjects: LCSH: Machine quilting. | Decoration and ornament--Themes, motives.

Classification: LCC TT835 .W356527 2017 | DDC 746.46--dc23

LC record available at https://lccn.loc.gov/2017006148

Printed in the USA

20 19 18 17 16 15 14 13 12

CONTENTS

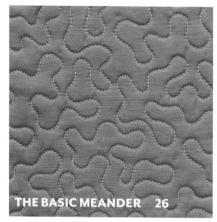

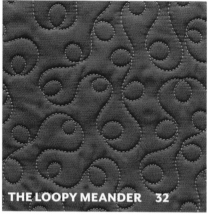

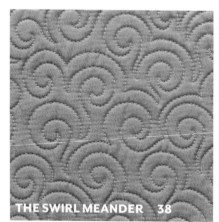

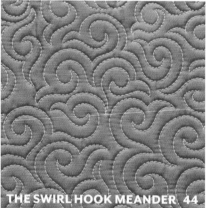

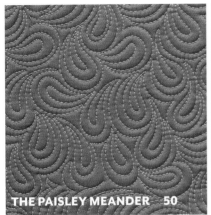
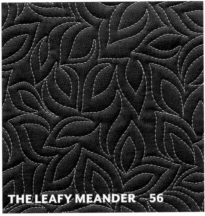
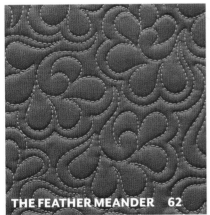

INTRODUCTION

The curse of knowledge is a real thing. Once a skill is learned, it is hard to remember not knowing how to do it. While it may be hard for me to remember what it was like to be a brand new machine quilter, I see it in the faces of my students when I teach machine quilting classes.

You're sitting at your sewing machine with a quilt top, ready to quilt. You know what you want the quilting to look like, but your hands won't cooperate. There's no doubt that it's a frustrating experience. But, I want to show you that, just like any other skill, it can be learned.

That's why I wrote this book. I learned machine quilting through trial and error, mostly error. I want to show you that finishing your own quilts isn't as hard as you might think.

Myth of Expertise

It can be tempting to think that there is a "correct" way to free-motion quilt, but that isn't the case. There are many, many different ways. As I always say, "I am not an expert in machine quilting, I am only the expert of my own opinion." In this book, I will share what works for me. Remember though, these are only suggestions. If something doesn't work for you, try something different!

Why Meanders?

A meander is a quilting design that is repeated to fill in an area. It's one of the most versatile designs to learn. A couple of meandering designs in your arsenal are all you need to quilt almost any quilt.

My only goal in this book is to encourage you to not only finish your quilts, but to actually enjoy the process. If you don't believe that it's possible, keep reading and I will do my best to convince you.

GETTING STARTED—THE BASICS

There are so many questions when it comes to machine quilting. Where to start? What to do? With so many options, it can be overwhelming. The most important thing is that you get started! That's why I am going to walk you through this step by step—almost as if I were sitting right next to you, drinking a coffee, and cheering you on.

We are not going to go over every option for every step of the process. Sometimes, having too many choices can make it harder to get started. Instead, I'm going to share what works for me. Then, as you become more familiar with machine quilting, you can experiment with different notions and tools. Getting started is the most important part of this process.

Tools Needed

Here are the very basic things you need to get started.

GET OFF ON THE RIGHT FOOT

To get started, you need a sewing machine and a free-motion quilting foot. This is the magic tool that makes free-motion quilting possible.

If you aren't sure what to use with your machine, check with your machine's manufacturer. It may be called a darning foot or hopping foot. There are several different types, just pick one and try it out. As you become more comfortable with free-motion quilting, you can try out different options to see what you prefer.

A sampling of free-motion quilting feet

DROP THE FEED DOGS

These guys get a break. Normally they move the fabric through while you sew, but since they pull in just one direction, they aren't ideal for free-motion quilting.

If your machine is older or won't let you drop the feed dogs, you can cover them with a Supreme Slider (page 11).

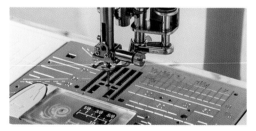

Feed dogs dropped

NOTE

You may think that you need a special machine to free-motion quilt your own quilt tops, but that isn't the case. Use the machine and the tools you already have and get started.

GRAB SOME QUALITY THREAD

When it comes to machine quilting, the thread is so very important. Trust me on this! Thread that works great for piecing won't necessarily work well for machine quilting. Moving the quilt in all different directions at different speeds will put stress on the thread. Using a high-quality thread will help prevent thread breaking and tension issues.

Thread

What does it all mean? Here are a couple of different things to consider when choosing the perfect thread (for you).

TYPE

There are so many different types of thread available. I could spend the rest of the book talking just about thread. (Don't worry, I won't.) The two most common types, polyester and cotton, are best for new machine quilters.

Polyester thread tends to be thinner and stronger than cotton thread. It has low lint and tends to blend into the quilt more than cotton.

The threads I use the most are So Fine! by Superior Threads (*left*) and Aurifil cotton (*right*).

Cotton thread tends to be a little thicker than polyester, which means you can see where you are going while quilting. It has a little more lint than poly thread but looks amazing on your quilts.

WEIGHT

The weight of a thread refers to how thick it is—the higher the number, the thinner the thread. Which weight you should use depends on how much you want the quilting to show up.

Starting with a 50-weight (or even a 40-weight) is a good option.

COLOR

This is the fun part; picking out the perfect color thread from the enormous selection available—there is no wrong answer. Pick what you think looks great.

Although I love a range of fun colors, I tend to use neutrals the most. Off-white, light yellow, gray, and tan are my most commonly used quilting threads. When the thread matches the fabric on the quilt top, it helps keep the quilting from overwhelming the quilt.

CHOOSE THE BATTING

Choosing the batting is an important part of the quilt-making process. The good thing is that, as long as you choose a quality batting, there is no wrong answer.

Batting

I prefer polyester batting because it has a nice drape and it resists creasing. Cotton batting is also a great option. It has an amazing softness and is perfect for bed quilts. Ultimately, the best option is to try all different kinds of batting and see what you prefer!

TIP *I like to use Quilters Dream Fusion fusible batting,* because it's machine-washable and won't gum up your needle while quilting. Other than being fusible, it's just like regular batting. ●

Try different kinds of batting and see what kind you prefer.

GRAB SOME NEEDLES

Q. **What about needles? Do I need a special needle?**

A. The short answer is no. I use the same universal needle for piecing and machine quilting. However, if you are using a specialty thread, or fabric other than cotton, you will probably want to use a different needle. Check the thread manufacturers suggestion for more guidance.

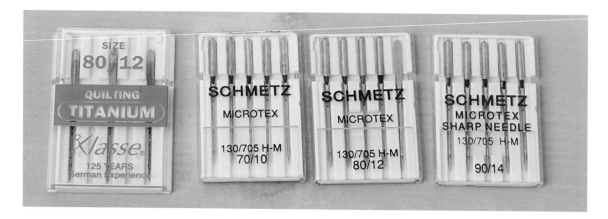

Optional Supplies

These are the tools I like to use when I am free-motion quilting. While you don't need these to get started, they are worth looking into purchasing.

EXTENDED BASE

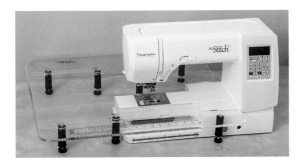

If your sewing machine manufacturer makes an extended base, you might want to consider getting one. It provides a bigger surface for the quilt, allowing you to quilt more easily. If you like machine quilting at all, this is the first thing I would suggest purchasing.

SUPREME SLIDER

I think the hardest part of machine quilting is dealing with the weight of the quilt. The Supreme Free-Motion Slider (by Pat LaPierre) is a Teflon sheet that allows you to move the quilt with less drag. I can hardly quilt without one!

GLOVES

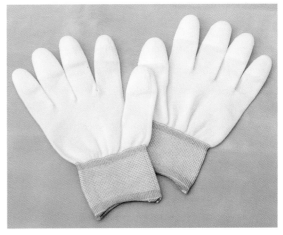

Having a good grip on your quilt will help you have more control during the quilting process. I like how they allow me to grab the quilt more easily. Some machine quilters swear by them and some can't stand them.

NOTE

There are tons of machine quilting tools and notions available on the market, too many to even discuss in a single book. It can be tempting to buy everything when you're starting out, but I always tell newer quilters to add to their stockpile slowly. The more you machine quilt, the more you will know what tools and notions will help you.

Get Your Quilt Ready

Now that your machine is ready, let's prepare the quilt sandwich. Layer the parts of the quilt and stabilize them, so you can easily move them as one. This is called "basting the quilt" in machine quilting lingo. Properly basting the layers of the quilt will help prevent any tucks on the back and makes the whole process a lot smoother.

Just like the rest of the machine quilting, there are a lot of different ways to baste your quilt sandwich. My favorite way to baste quilts is with fusible batting.

Fusible batting is just like regular batting, except that one side has a thin layer of fusible glue on it that is activated when you iron it. It's quick and I like not having to worry about running into pins while I quilt.

···················· STEP ONE ····················

Lay the backing face down on a flat surface.

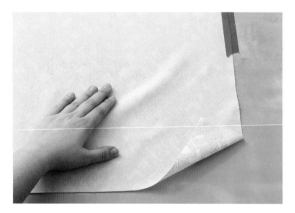

Smooth out any wrinkles and try to get the backing as flat as possible. To keep it in place and extra taunt, you can tape the sides down. Just be sure that the tape won't hurt your floor!

NOTE

I like to make my backing a couple inches bigger than the quilt top on all sides.

The extra fabric gives me something to hold onto when I am quilting along the edge.

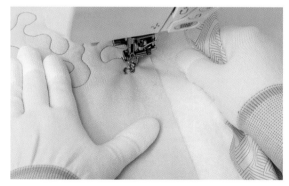

Place the fusible batting onto the backing (see Batting, page 10).

Quilters Dream Fusion recommends that you lay the batting with the glue side up. (Be sure to follow the instructions on your batting.) Again, smooth the batting making sure there are no bumps or wrinkles.

STEP THREE

Spread the quilt top on the batting.

NOTE

Having a properly prepared quilt top will help you enjoy the quilting process as much as possible. Make sure there are no holes in the top and that the seams are pressed.

Smooth it out, getting the top nice and flat. Can you tell that this is important? Trust me, spending a little extra time to ensure that all the layers are nice and flat will prevent frustration when you start quilting. When it comes to machine quilting, the fewer bumps the better.

STEP FOUR

Use a hot, dry iron to iron the top from the center out.

Make sure not to touch the iron to the batting. If you do, you will end up with a gooey mess. Don't rush through this step. You want all the fusible glue to melt and adhere the layers together.

There you have it, a quilt sandwich that looks good enough to eat ... or at least good enough to quilt. Let's get started!

FIRST STITCHES

Let's Quilt!

Woo-hoo! This is it, the moment we have been working up to. Don't be nervous, it's going to be fun.

For now, let's get comfortable with moving the quilt around while machine quilting. Don't worry about anything else right now ... not stitch length or what it looks like. I like to say that worrying about the stitch length when learning how to quilt is like writing a novel while you are learning your letters. It's something we will learn ... just not right now.

NOTE

For the best results, in the very beginning, start with a smaller quilt project. In my classes, I have students bring a fat quarter quilt sandwich. It's perfect for letting you get comfortable with the machine and moving the fabric, without having to deal with the drag of a large quilt.

· STEP ONE ·

Place the quilt sandwich under the needle.

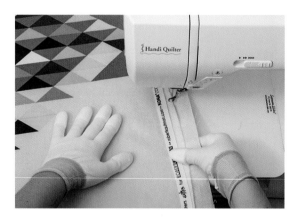

NOTE

One of the benefits of quilting on a sewing machine is that you can start wherever you like. Most of the time, I start in the center of the quilt. The reasoning is purely psychological. I know that the quilt will never be harder to move than it is at that moment. But that's just what works for me, start wherever you want.

Secure the beginning of the line of stitching by taking a few small stitches in place.

I try to start my line of quilting in a seam or on a busier print. It helps to hide the stitches.

Pull the bobbin thread up to the top to prevent any knots or loose thread on the back.
It's not hard to do. It just takes a few steps.

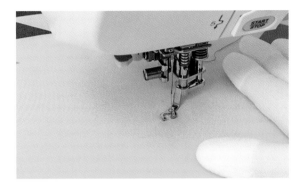

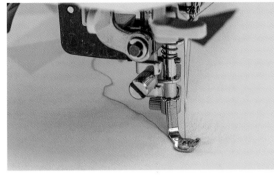

1 Lower the foot.

2 Make one stitch, leaving the needle in the up position.

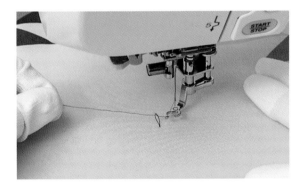

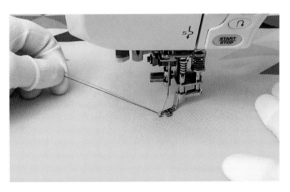

3 Holding onto the "tail" of the top thread, raise the foot and move the quilt sandwich over slightly. The bobbin thread should pull up.

4 Hold both the top thread and the bobbin thread. Move the quilt so the needle is directly over where the bobbin thread is coming up.

5 Quilt a few small stitches in place to secure the quilting.

I feel that this is enough to secure the quilting. But if you are worried it will unravel, you can add a few drops of fabric glue to secure it.

Start quilting.

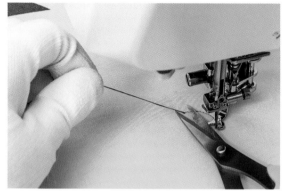

1 Press the pedal down and start quilting. Try quilting your name, moving around, whatever. At this point just try getting used to moving the fabric.

2 Once you have quilted a couple of inches, stop, then trim off the tail threads from your securing stitches. Get in the habit of doing this now to prevent the threads from accidentally getting stuck in the stitches.

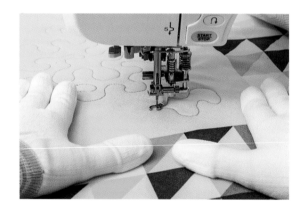

3 Keep moving the fabric around as you begin to be comfortable with the whole process.

NOTE

Here's where I get a little "new age-y." As you quilt, try to close your brain off to quilting. Don't judge how you are doing, don't worry about the stitch length or anything else. Instead, try to think of nothing, or of anything else. If possible, try to enjoy just moving your hands around. This is machine quilting at its most basic and I think it's awesomely fun.

Secure the end of the line of stitching by taking a few small stitches in place.

You can just cut the threads, or you can bring the bobbin thread up to the top. It takes a couple extra steps, but it prevents having any loose threads on the back. Either way is completely fine!

Here's how I like to secure the end of the line of quilting when I am finished.

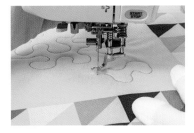 

1 Take a few tiny stitches in place.

2 Raise the needle and the foot.

3 Move the quilt sandwich over to one side and grab the top thread.

 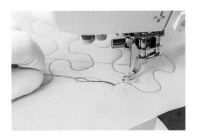 

4 Bring the quilt back so that the needle is over the point where the thread comes out of the quilt top. Loop the top thread around your finger.

5 Raise the foot and move the quilt over, so the bobbin thread comes up.

6 Trim both threads, so they are flush with the quilt top.

Now take that sample and frame it! It's your first machine-quilted sample (or at least one of your first attempts). You are doing your best quilting right now, be proud of it. By the time you have worked your way through the book, you will have already improved.

NOTE

Use the hand wheel or a needle up/down button when making the stitches that secure the quilting. You don't want to use the pedal because you may take too many. We don't want any fingers harmed when quilting.

Frequently Asked Questions (FAQs) ········▶

Now that you have quilted a little bit, I am sure you have some questions. Hopefully one of them isn't, "Why on earth am I trying this?" As we continue through the designs, hopefully I will have answered most, if not all, of your quilting questions. For now I will address some of the most frequently asked questions in my classes.

Q. Where should my hands go?

A. *You will have the most control of your quilting when you hands are on either side of the needle, about 3 or 4 inches away.*

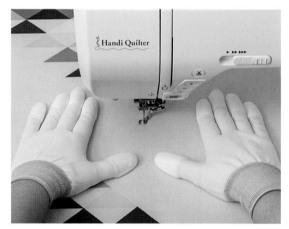

Proper hand placement will give you the most control of your quilting.

As you quilt, be sure to reposition your hands often. Forgetting to reposition my hands is my worst habit. I will be quilting along and realize that my hands are way over to one side. It's hard to have good control when your hands aren't in the proper place.

Q. How fast should I quilt?

A. *It depends. (I know it isn't probably the answer you want). The best speed is one that isn't so slow that you can critique the job you're doing while you're doing it, but not a speed so fast that you feel out of control. The speed you use will change as you get more comfortable with quilting, so don't be afraid to change the settings.*

NOTE

Your sewing machine may come with a stitch regulator, which means that it will speed up or slow down depending on how fast you move the quilt sandwich. If your machine has one, you don't have to worry about what speed to use.

In the beginning, adjust your needle speed (if your machine has one) to a speed that allows you to put your foot pedal all the way down. (Unless you have a stitch regulator.) Not having to think about the position of your foot gives your mind one less thing to worry about.

If your stitches are too large, speed up the machine. If they are too small, slow the speed.

Make the speed of the machine fit the movement of your hands not the other way around.

Q. Ack! Should I be making the stitches all the same length?

A. *Consistent stitch length comes with practice. The more comfortable you become with a particular machine quilting design, the easier it will be to keep the stitch length consistent. Worrying about it right now will only drive you crazy.*

Q. How should I sit at the machine?

A. *Make sure that your chair and table is the right height for you. You don't want to be hunched over or reaching up, it will hurt your back.*

Q. What should I do if the bobbin runs out?

A. *Ahhh … the dreaded empty bobbin. It always seems to run out just when you are getting into your quilting groove. When the bobbin runs out, I start by trimming any loose threads. When I start the new line of quilting, I overlap it by an inch or so. It helps secure the stitching.*

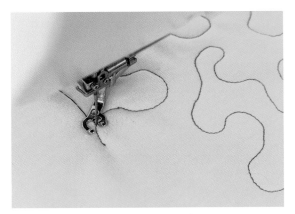

Overlap the new line of quilting by an inch to secure the first line.

Q. Why is the tension off on my quilting?

A. *If all of the quilting has poor tension, it may mean that you need to adjust the tension of the thread on the machine. If it is intermittently messing up, it could be that you aren't moving at a consistent speed. As you get more comfortable with a design, you may notice that the tension improves.*

TIPS *Proper Tension*

There is no denying that tension is one of the most frustrating parts of machine quilting. If you find your tension is off, here are a few steps to take.

1. Rethread the machine. This is the absolute first thing that I do when problems arise. You don't want to adjust the tension, only to find that the machine wasn't threaded correctly.

2. Check for fuzz or lint in the bobbin or thread path.

3. Change the needle. A dull needle can affect the tension the quilting. Either try a new needle or a different type of needle.

4. Make sure that the thread is quality thread. Again, the thread that works for piecing isn't necessarily good for machine quilting. ●

BUILDING BLOCKS

Now that you are familiar with the very basics of moving the quilt,
let's focus on getting more comfortable with machine quilting.

Practice, Practice, Practice

As much as I hate to say it, there is only one way to get better at machine quilting ... practice.

You can read books, look at tutorials, and watch videos, but ultimately you need to actually quilt. Before you shut the book and use it as a doorstop, I have some good news. It doesn't take as much practice as you might think. You don't need to practice a lot, you just need to practice productively.

PRODUCTIVE PRACTICE

"Practice makes perfect," is a phrase I am sure you have heard before. It's a nice saying, but I don't agree. I think that *productive* practice makes better quilters. Being deliberate about how you practice will make a world of difference in your quilting.

Next time you get ready to machine quilt, try following these steps.

1 *Pick one thing to improve.*

....

Each time you quilt, whether on a quilt or just a practice piece, pick one thing you want to improve. (Yes, only one thing.) Trying to improve everything at once is a surefire way to overwhelm yourself or become discouraged. You could work on:

• Keeping the stitch length consistent

• Getting comfortable with the basic shape of the design

• Finding the perfect speed

• Not cussing while quilting (Hey, it doesn't matter what your goal is, just that you have one!)

Building Blocks

2 *Once you have identified your one thing, start quilting, focusing only on that thing.*

....

3 *Assess how you did.*

....

When you are finished, look it over and see how you did. But here's the trick, try not to assess while quilting. Wait until you are finished and look over the whole area you quilted, not just up close.

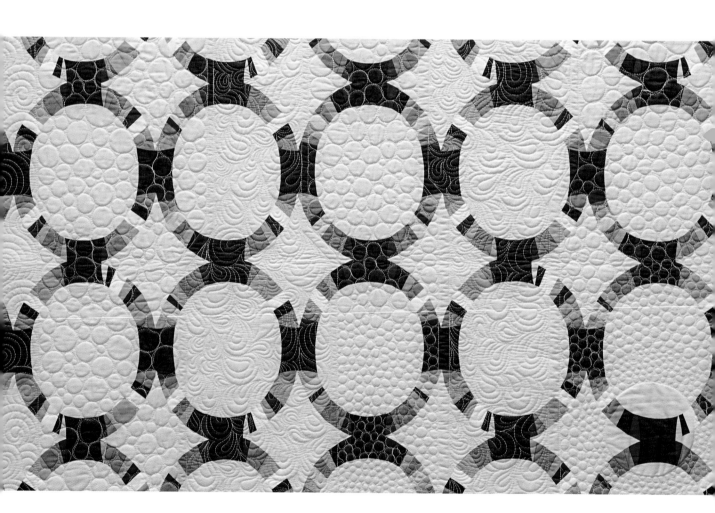

4 *Celebrate the successes.*

Look for what you did right. When I was first learning how to machine quilt, something I would tell myself often was, "Well, it's not as crappy as last time."

5 *Refine and repeat.*

If there are areas that need improvement, make a mental note of what you could do differently and work on it again next time. What I really want you to remember is this, be self-aware without judgment. Talk to yourself as though you are talking to a friend about their quilting.

6 *Track your progress.*

Having a visual reminder of your improvement will keep you motivated and encouraged. If you are working on practice samples, put the date next to the quilting. I promise, you'll see improvement after even just a few practice sessions.

7 *Enjoy the process.*

As impossible as it may sound, try to enjoy the learning process. Instead of chasing an unattainable goal, you are on a journey. Try to enjoy each step and each "win" you make. I know it sounds cheesy, but it's true.

My hope is that productive practice will help keep you focused on improving and not on what you're doing wrong.

Okay, now let's start quilting some of my favorite quilting designs!

THE MEANDERS

Ready to get started? Everything in this book has led us to this point—learning some meanders to put on your quilts. There are so many different machine-quilting designs you can learn, but I am going to share my favorites.

These designs are versatile and can be used on many different kinds of quilts, from modern to traditional. Each of the meander designs builds on the previous one—they start out easy, then become a little more challenging. If you have already sneaked a peek at the designs in the book, don't be overwhelmed. By the time you have worked through all the designs, it will become a natural progression.

NOTE
Drawing is great practice too!

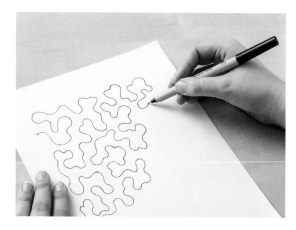

Let's face it, sometimes real life intrudes into our quilting time. If you can't get to your sewing machine as much as you'd like, grab a pen and some paper instead; 80% of quilting is knowing where you are going. Drawing out a design will help you learn it almost as well as quilting it.

The Ultimate Challenge

Before we start, I'd like to pose a challenge for you. I promise, it's nothing too crazy.

Quilt a square and fill it in. That's it. See, it's not that scary.

Here's what I want you to do:

1 Sew a line of stitches to make a square.

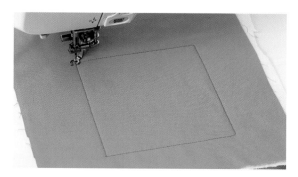

It doesn't actually have to be a square; it can be any shape. You just need to have a defined area.

2 Fill in the square with the quilting design you are practicing.

Don't stop until it's filled in, don't critique how it looks, and definitely do not take out the quilting.

WHY DO THIS?

It's one thing to know how to quilt a design, but it's a completely different thing to know how to maneuver around an area and fill it in completely. Filling in a defined space will help you learn how to do just that, while practicing a new design.

In each chapter I will show you how to quilt a different meander design and demonstrate how to fill in a square completely with the design.

Most importantly, doing this will help you realize that mistakes aren't as noticeable when the whole area is filled in completely.

Mistakes

While quilting you might make a mistake. (Not that I think you would make a mistake, you look very smart ... this is just a hypothetical situation.)

This mistake is very noticeable when it's by itself. In fact, you might be tempted to take it out. But you can't take rip out the quilting because, according to the challenge, you have to keep quilting.

Once the mistake is surrounded by quilting, it is far less noticeable.

Can you imagine how much less noticeable it would be if I was using a thread color that matched the fabric?

The moral of the story is, when you make a mistake, don't rip it out. Just throw more quilting around it. At least, that's what I do.

THE BASIC MEANDER

First up, the basic meander. This design is so great, it's a noun and a verb. "Let's start meandering with the meander." See what I mean? It's perfect to start with because it's made up of only gentle curves. There is no traveling, echoing, or changing direction.

Learning how to quilt smooth, curvy lines is the first step to learning the rest of the designs in this book.

TIP *Don't turn the quilt sandwich as you quilt.* Use your hands to move it in all different directions, but don't actually rotate the quilt. Spinning the quilt around is easy enough on a small project but is much harder to do on a larger quilt. Don't develop the habit now and you will thank me later. ●

Quilting the Basic Meander

TIP *My favorite visual for this design is to imagine a river winding all through the area.* When quilting the meander, always move in a forward motion. Just like a river, there is no backing up. ●

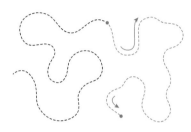

1 Starting in any area of the block, begin quilting a curvy line.

2 Continue quilting a line that curves in all different directions, trying to keep the line as smooth as possible.

3 Focus on making yourself stitch in all different directions; up, down, left, and right.

4 Don't worry about how curvy the line is, instead, focus on keeping the spacing between the lines as consistent as possible.

TIPS *Keep in Mind*

· Going in all different directions will help make the quilting look random. The more random the design, the better it will look. Anytime the pattern is noticeable, it detracts from the overall texture of the design.

· Don't forget to reposition your hands as you quilt. If your machine has a setting for needle down position, have it set so it stops with the needle down. This will allow you to move your hands while the quilt stays in place. ●

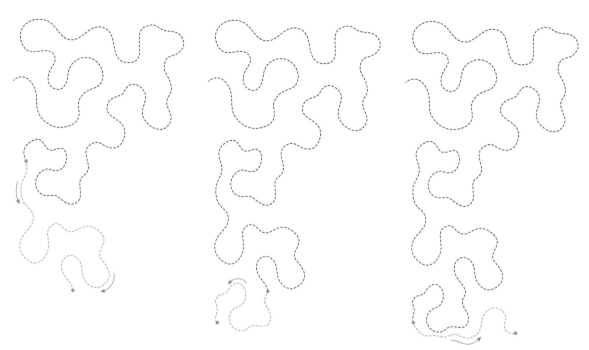

If you are stuck in a corner, try quilting along the edge of the block to get out.

5 Keep quilting the meandering line, filling in the area completely.

TIP *The hardest part of learning any new design is trying to keep from getting stuck in an area.* If you find your quilting line trapped, just quilt your way back out. You could travel over a previously quilted line or in between other lines. It may look noticeable at first, but it will blend in more when the whole quilt is finished. ●

6 Don't forget to make the lines curvy or wavy. Doing so will add to the texture of the quilting and make it look good, even if it isn't perfect.

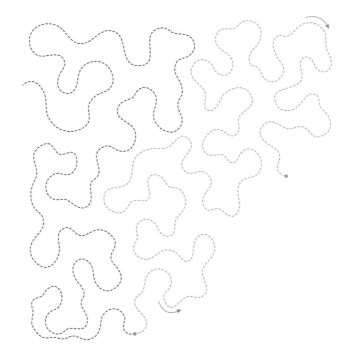

7 Fill in the whole block with the meander design.

If you don't love it, no worries! Start over and try again.

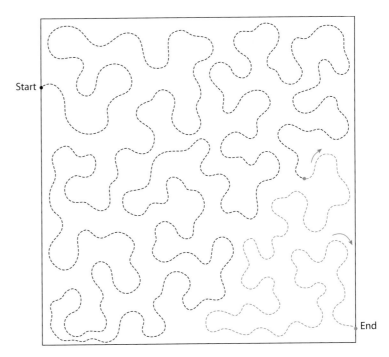

Other Ways to Use the Basic Meander

These sections show you different ways to use the quilting designs you have learned. Don't let this intimidate you. If you aren't ready, just come back to these sections later!

Once you can meander without fear, try shrinking it down. A basic meander quilted on a smaller scale is called stipple. Stippling is a great way to highlight areas on your quilt, or even other quilting designs.

Troubleshooting FAQs ···▶

Q. How can I make myself go in all different directions? I seem to get stuck going in one way.

A. *Our brains love repetition so it's completely normal to only move in one direction. Instead of getting frustrated, try giving yourself a different routine to follow. For instance, quilt the meandering line up, right, down, then right and repeat. You will still be following a routine but it will look much more random on the quilt.*

Q. How much space should I leave between the lines?

A. *Try leaving about ½˝ between the lines. Quilting the meander on a larger scale will give your mind some time to think through the next steps. Once you learn the design, you can practice quilting it on a smaller scale if you'd like.*

Practice quilting the meander, and see if you can get comfortable with moving around the defined area. Don't forget to breathe!

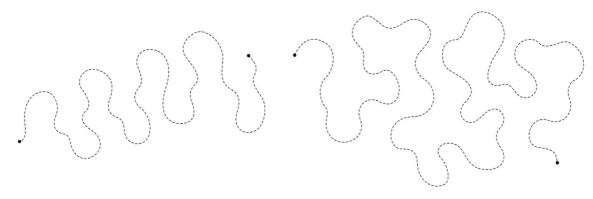

If your quilting looks too repetitive (*left*), try going in all different directions.

THE LOOPY MEANDER

Now that we have worked through the basic meander design, let's start building on it. The loopy meander still uses the same meandering line. The only difference is that you randomly add a small loop. That's all. There's nothing scary about loops, so don't be worried. In fact, I think they are adorable. It's a fun, whimsical design that is great for all kinds of quilts, especially for kids' quilts or novelty quilts.

Quilting the loopy meander will help you get comfortable with moving the fabric in all different directions. This will be helpful as you progress into the other designs in this book.

Quilting the Loopy Meander

1 Start by quilting the meandering line just as you did in the basic meander (page 27).

2 At a random moment—whenever you are ready—quilt a loop shape. This loop can happen anywhere in the design.

TIP *When you quilt a loop, you are trying to quilt a circular shape.* Please notice that I said "circular," but I could have just as easily said "circle-ish." It doesn't have to be a perfect circle, it can be a teardrop or any other shape you feel like quilting. ●

3 Once the loop is finished, continue on the path of the meandering line. It should look as though, if the loop were removed, the line would still look fine.

4 Continue quilting the meandering line, adding another loop when you are ready.

The loops can go in any direction, so don't overthink that part of the design.

TIP *If quilting loops makes you nervous, just add a few throughout the area.* Adding them in slowly will help make learning them less overwhelming. Remember, there is no rush. Learn at your own pace. ●

The loop can be any size. If you want the loops to be the most noticeable part of the design, quilt them bigger.

If you want the loops to blend in with the meander or not be as noticeable, quilt them smaller. This would be the way to quilt it if you are new to machine quilting and don't want any of the mistakes to be noticeable.

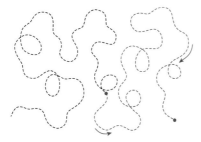

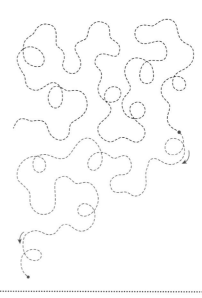

5 Once you are comfortable quilting the loops, try adding more of them to the meander line.

Don't forget to quilt the line in all different directions.

6 As you quilt, add as few or as many loops as you like. Make this design fit your preferences.

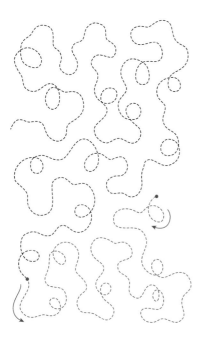

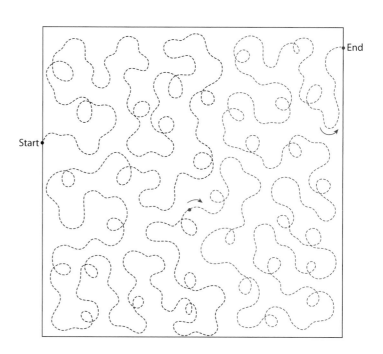

7 Continue quilting loops and meandering until you fill the area.

The most important thing is that the area is filled in as completely as possible. No one will notice that your loops aren't perfect. All they will see is the overall texture of the design.

Other Ways to Use the Loopy Meander

Once you have mastered the loopy meander, try using it in different ways on your quilts.

AS A BORDER DESIGN

This design is perfect for thinner borders and sashing. This is also a great way to practice quilting loops, if the thought of filling in a whole area seems daunting. You can also change the orientation of the loops or quilt them all facing the same direction.

Loops alternating
directions

Loops going the
same direction

ADD MORE LOOPS

Sometimes, more is better. To make this meander even more loopy, quilt two loops instead of one. I like to quilt it almost like a figure eight.

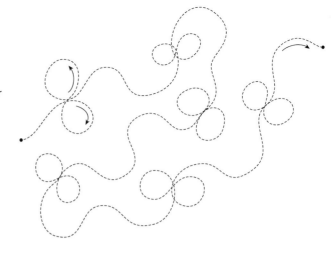

Troubleshooting FAQs ····▶

Q. Why do my loops look pointy?

A. *If you are having a hard time getting your loops to look round, you might try to move a little faster. Quilting slowly doesn't create momentum, which is what helps you create nice, smooth curves.*

Q. What if I get stuck?

A. *Since this design has crossing lines, it's easy to maneuver your way out if you are stuck. Just quilt more loopy lines. Even if they cross over your previous quilting, it won't be that noticeable.*

● *Are you ready to get a little loopy with your quilts? Try quilting it and see how easy it is to move the quilt in all different directions.* ●

THE SWIRL MEANDER

What you'll master:
Echoing

Swirls are my absolute favorite quilting design. From traditional to modern, novelty to art, I have never seen a quilt that wouldn't look great quilted with swirls. After a little practice, I think you will love swirls as much as I do!

This is the first design to incorporate echoing, which is an important skill to learn. I always say that echoing is your friend, in fact, it's your best friend. Echo quilting allows you to maneuver around an area and helps you learn to change direction with your quilting—both of which are useful skills for future quilting designs

Quilting the Swirl Meander

NOTE

NOTE

Echoing is quilting the same shape as a prior quilted line, with a space between. Most often, echo quilting is done outside of a design, but can also be quilted inside the design.

1 Start by quilting the beginning of a swirl; a line that curls in on itself.

The first part of the swirl doesn't have to be large. Try quilting it about the size of a quarter. Make sure to leave yourself room to work your way back out in the next step.

2 Finish the swirl by echoing back around the first line, stopping before you touch anything.

There isn't any touching in this design. As soon as you come close the edge of the area or another swirl, stop and quilt your next swirl.

TIP *Don't forget to finish the swirl.* It's the most important part of this design. It won't look horrible; it's just not the look that we are going for. If your swirls start looking like that, don't stop quilting or rip it out. Just keep going, trying to remember to finish the swirls as you go. ●

3 Quilt another little swirl, then echo around it, stopping before you touch the previously quilted swirl.

4 Third time's a charm! Quilt another swirl.

TIP *Remember, there is no touching in this design.* As you start to approach another swirl or the edge of an area, it's time to change direction. ●

If you forget to "finish your swirls," your quilting may look like this.

TIP *You may notice that some of my swirls face down, and some face up.* That's how it is supposed to be! The swirls can point in any direction.

Both versions look great! So don't worry about the direction, just quilt a swirl and finish it. ●

Swirls all facing same direction

Swirls facing different directions

5 Echo the swirl.

It's time to include echoing in our design. Echoing around your swirls is the perfect way to maneuver your way around the area. You can echo the swirl you just quilted.

Or you could echo a previously quilted swirl.

TIP *Keeping the spacing of the echo lines the same as the swirls* will help them blend in with the rest of the quilting. ●

6 Continue quilting swirls and echoing.

7 To fill in any corners or small gaps, you can quilt a smaller swirl.

Or you can add more echo lines.

If you get stuck, you can travel along the edge of the areas.

Just like all the other designs, it's more important that it's filled in completely than if it's perfect.

8 When in doubt, echo. You can even echo around the whole group of swirls. This will help you move into areas that you need to fill in.

9 If there isn't enough room to echo around the whole swirl, just go until you run out of room and then change direction.

10 Keep echoing and swirling until the whole area is filled in.

TIP *There are only two steps to this design—swirl and echo.* As you are quilting, if you become confused, just remember to pick one. There is no wrong answer! Breaking a design down to its most basic elements will help keep it from being overwhelming. ●

Other Ways to Use the Swirl Meander

Quilting the swirl on a smaller scale is a great way to turn an allover design into filler. Filler quilting designs are used to highlight blocks or even other quilting designs.

In fact, all the designs in this book can be quilted as fillers by shrinking them.

Troubleshooting FAQs ··· ▶

Q. My swirls look more square than round, what am I doing wrong?

A. *Congratulations! If your swirls look more like squares than circles, you are almost there. As you become more comfortable with this, or any design, you will be able to move faster and more consistently which leads to nice, round swirls. Keep it up!*

Q. Does it matter what size I make the first part of the swirl?

A. *No. Just as with any design, the spacing between the lines determines the how dense the quilting is. To have swirls that look the same size, focus on the distance between the lines.*

Q. I'm following the steps, but it doesn't look right. How can I improve them?

A. *The most common mistake is making the swirls more long than round. Quilting them so that they are round, almost like a circle, will help prevent any irregularly shaped gaps between the swirls.*

Instead of making the swirls long (*left*), aim for making them round (*right*).

Q. Why are my swirls all going in a row?

A. *If your swirls are in a line, it means that you aren't echoing enough. Echoing around the swirls allows you to go in all different directions.*

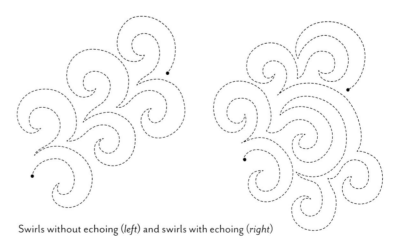

Swirls without echoing (*left*) and swirls with echoing (*right*)

THE SWIRL HOOK MEANDER

What you'll master:
echoing individual parts of a design

The swirl hook design takes a basic swirl and adds another little step, a hook. It's great for irregular shaped areas or between blocks, and I especially like it for masculine quilts. No matter how you choose to use it, it's definitely a design worth learning.

The swirl hook meander still incorporates echoing and changing directions. But now we are echoing different parts of the swirl. Don't let it overwhelm you. I will break down the design to make it as easy as possible. You will master the swirl hook meander in no time!

Quilting the Swirl Hook Meander

1 Quilt the beginning of a swirl, just as you did with the swirl meander (page 39).

2 Quilt a serpentine line as a hook extending from the curl.

It doesn't matter how long or short the hook is or even how curvy it is. Just quilt an "S" shape that extends from the swirl.

3 Echo the hook back toward the swirl, stopping about ½˝ from the swirl.

This is where most quilters get tripped up. You don't have to rethink the design, just echo around what you have already quilted. Sometimes we tend to make the quilting harder than it has to be.

TIP *If echoing around the hook is tripping you up, you can just quilt the hook and then echo around the swirl.* Leaving that step out will give you one less thing to think about. ●

4 Now, echo around the rest of the swirl, stopping before you run into anything.

In this step, we are finishing the swirl, just as we did in the swirl meander.

5 Quilt the beginning of another swirl.

Just as with the swirl meander, it doesn't matter what direction the swirl faces. Just quilt another swirl close to the previously quilted one.

6 Quilt another hook.

Try to keep the serpentine line close to other swirls. It will help prevent gaps in the quilting.

7 Finish the swirl by echoing the hook and then echoing around the swirl.

8 Quilt your next complete swirl hook.

9 Echo around a swirl.

Just like the swirl design, echoing is an easy way to maneuver your way around the area. You can echo the swirl that you just quilted or even one quilted previously, as I did here.

TIP *Echoing is also a great way to deal with the corners of an area.* If you can't fit the whole design, just echo the lines you have already quilted until it's filled in.

Then, when you have room, you can quilt your next swirl. ●

Continue quilting swirl hooks and echoing to fill in the complete area.

TIP *If quilting the hooks in this design seem a little difficult, start by adding a few swirl hooks in among some basic swirls.* It will let you practice a little bit without feeling overwhelmed by a new design.

Focus on keeping the spacing consistent. Instead of focusing on the hook or the swirls, pay attention to the spacing between the lines. If the spacing is consistent, it gives the illusion of perfection. ●

Other Ways to Use the Swirl Hook Meander

COMBINE WITH THE SWIRL MEANDER

Add the swirl meander. You don't have to add hooks to every swirl. Try adding them to just a few of the swirls until you get the hang of the design.

AS A BORDER DESIGN

I love using this swirl hook design in borders that are 3˝–5˝ wide. It's a great way to practice the hook in a more confined space.

Quilting the swirl hook in alternating directions really fills in the area nicely.

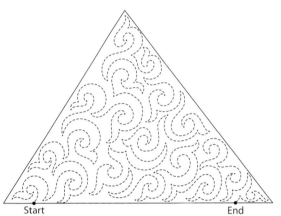

Start   End

····· *Troubleshooting FAQs* ····▶

Q. Why is the hook giving me so much trouble?

A. *The "hook" part of this design looks easy but quilting it can be a little tricky. The "S" shape of the hook is stitched between the two steps of quilting a swirl and switching between the two can get overwhelming. If you just can't seem to get the hang of it, try tracing the illustrations in this chapter as many times as it takes to get comfortable with the shape. Once you get the hang of the shape, try quilting it.*

Q. Why do I have gaps in between my swirls?

A. *While you are quilting, be sure to keep the hooks close to other swirls. Doing this will help fill in any little gaps as you quilt.*

Keeping hooks close to the swirl

Hooks not close to the swirl

THE PAISLEY MEANDER

The paisley meander is such a beautiful design and it works on all sorts of quilts. You can use it as an allover design, but it works just as well as a background filler. Try quilting it around blocks, appliqué, or even quilted motifs.

What you'll master:
Directional quilting designs

With this design, we are still sticking with the curviness of the swirls that we have learned. The only difference is now we will be thinking about the direction of our design. Swirls aren't directional; that means that you can quilt the design in any way that you would like. But with paisleys, changing the direction of the design is key to creating a nice overall texture.

Quilting the Paisley Meander

NOTE

Your paisleys may be curved like mine, or they may be straighter. Either way is perfect!

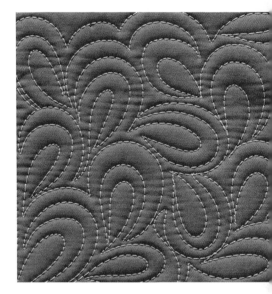

1 Start by quilting a line that goes out and curves back to where you started. It is almost like a teardrop shape. It should be rounded at one end and come to a point at the other.

2 Echo around the paisley, going around the curved end and coming back to the pointed end.

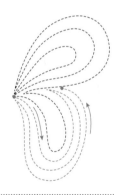

3 Echo a third time. In fact, you can echo the paisley as many times as you would like.

The echo lines don't have to perfectly touch at the points, just get them as close as you can.

4 Quilt another teardrop shape that extends from the pointed end of the first paisley.

5 Echo the paisley 2 or 3 times.

NOTE

Notice that you can't always get back to the pointed end of the paisley. That's completely fine. Just get as close as you can and then change direction and echo again.

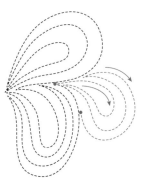

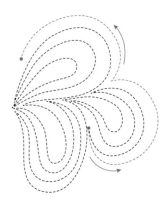

6 Quilt another paisley with the echo lines.

7 If needed, echo around a previously quilted paisley.

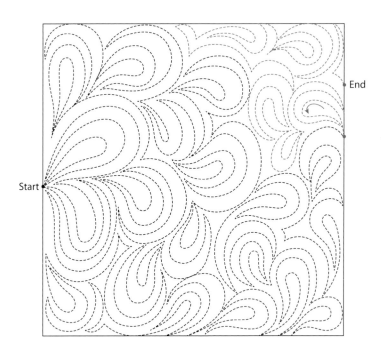

Echoing around other paisleys will help you maneuver around the area.

Fill in the area by quilting paisleys and echo lines.

- When quilting in the corners and other irregularly shaped areas, be sure to fill the area as much as possible, even if you aren't able to echo around the whole paisley.

- Don't be afraid to extend the first part of the paisley out from the rest of the quilting. Doing that will leave enough space for the echo lines.

- If you get stuck, just quilt your way out. Whether you quilt along another line or squeeze out between lines, it will look fine. I promise, when the whole quilt is finished, you won't even notice it.

- There might be times when you find yourself stuck between two paisleys, without room to add another one. If that happens, echo quilt until you fill in the area and move to where you have room to add the next paisley.

Tips continue on next page

- Filling in the space as consistently as possible is probably the most difficult part of any quilting design. A good rule of thumb is that as long as a gap is smaller than the individual design, it won't be noticeable.

Since this gap is smaller than the paisley, I am fine with just leaving it alone. Of course, you could fill it in with more echoes if you prefer.

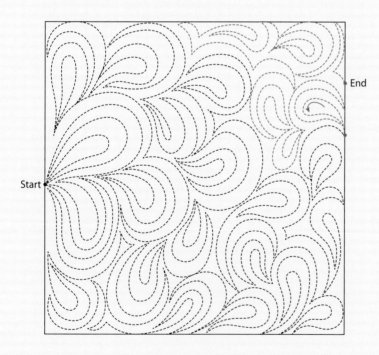

- Fill in the area by quilting paisleys and echo lines.

Other Ways to Use the Paisley Meander

Once you get comfortable with the paisley meander, you can use it to highlight other areas of your quilt. For instance, quilting paisleys around a block or appliqué is a fun way to give your quilting a more custom look.

Paisleys highlighting an appliqué block

•••••• Troubleshooting FAQs •••▶

Q. Why are all my paisleys going the same way?

A. *Don't forget the echoing! Echoing around previously quilted paisleys will make it easier to go in all different directions.*

Q. Do all the paisleys have to be the same size?

A. *Definitely not! In fact, changing up the sizes of your paisleys can add a fun look to your quilting.*

THE LEAFY MEANDER

Leaves are such a fun option for your quilts! Whether you want to add some detail to a landscape quilt, or just want to keep building on your previous designs, this one is for you.

So far, we have talked about working our way around an area, changing directions, and echoing. Now, we are going to add one more thing to think about—points. Quilting sharp points will help you learn how to control the movement of your quilt. I'll show you just how easy it can be.

Quilting the Leafy Meander

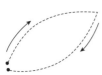
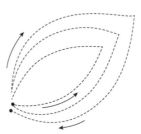
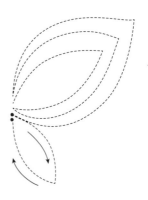

1 Quilt a line that arcs to a point and then arcs away and back to where you started.

It doesn't have to be perfectly symmetrical, or even very round—just make a somewhat pointy shape; it will be fine.

TIP *To get nice, sharp points, quilt into the point and quickly change direction to quilt the next side.* If you hesitate in the point of the leaf, you may have extra stitches in that area. It's not horrible, just something to keep an eye out for. ●

2 Echo the leaf.

By now you know what a fan I am of echoing, and this design has a lot of it! Echo the leaf just as you did the paisley (page 51), leaving a space between the points on one end and bringing them closer together at the other end.

NOTE
There is no set rule on how many times you should echo the leaf. Just echo a few times until you are ready to move on to the next leaf.

3 Quilt the next leaf, so it is facing in a different direction.

Quilting the leaves in different directions will keep the design looking random.

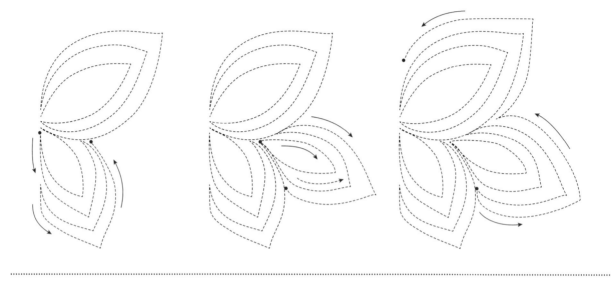

4 Echo around the second leaf 2 or 3 times.

NOTE

The echo lines don't have to touch at the bottom of each leaf. If you run out of room just change direction and quilt your next echo line.

5 Quilt another leaf and echo around it.

6 Just like the rest of the designs, you can echo previously quilted leaves.

This helps make it easier to point your leaves in different directions.

7 Continue filling in the area.

TIPS *Here are a few tips that will make quilting the design easier:*

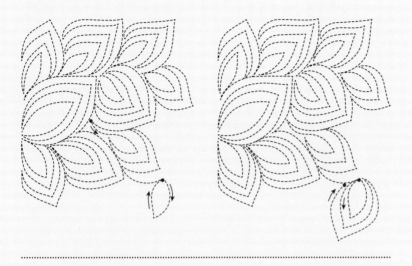

- Instead of starting a new leaf at the bottom of the previous one, you can quilt an echo line to the point of a previous leaf and then start the next one. This is helpful if you need to need to change directions quickly or quilt leaves in a small area.

- Each leaf doesn't have to be closed off at the bottom. If you run out of room or need to change direction quickly, quilt the leaf so it goes out to a point and then runs into another leaf.

- The leaves don't have to be the same size. If you can't fit a full-size leaf in an area, you can make them smaller. Just try to keep the spacing between the lines consistent.

Other Ways to Use the Leafy Meander

These leaves can actually make fun flower-like designs when quilted in a different arrangement. I especially like using it in square quilt blocks.

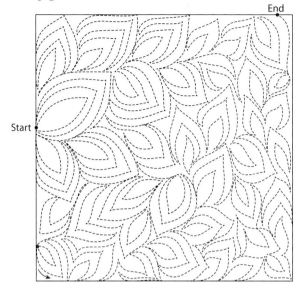

····· Troubleshooting FAQs ···▶

Q. Does it matter if my leaves are all different shapes?

A. *It doesn't matter at all! Just like handwriting, we all have our different style. You shouldn't try to make yours look just like mine. Just keep quilting and your own style will develop.*

Q. Why does one side of my leaf look different from the other?

A. *Congratulations, you are completely normal. Most people have a dominant side, which means one part of a design looks better than the other. Instead of being discouraged, take it as a sign that you are on the right track.*

Q. Why is the thread tension worse on parts of my leaves?

A. *Moving smoothly from curved lines to sharp points is something that gets easier with practice. If you find that only part of the leaves, such as the points, have poor tension, try to move in a smoother motion.*

THE FEATHER MEANDER

Feathers are the one quilting design that I really, really wanted to learn when I first started quilting. It took a lot of practice, but I finally figured it out. This meander takes a feather quilting design and makes it a little more manageable by only quilting one side. Once you're comfortable quilting this design, you will practically be ready for quilting full feathers in all areas of your quilts.

The feather meander incorporates traveling for the first time in this book. Traveling is quilting directly on a previously quilted line. It can seem a little daunting, but don't let it worry you. We are only using it in small increments.

Quilting the Feather Meander

One petal

Several petals around shape

Finished feather

1 Start by quilting a swirl shape (page 39), leaving at least ½˝ between the lines.

The swirl doesn't have to be any particular size, just make sure that there is enough space in between the lines to add the petals.

2 From the center of the swirl, begin quilting petal shapes.

NOTE

The petal shape is similar to a "half-heart" shape if we were to stretch out the swirl and lay it straight.

The petal should curve out and back, almost as if to merge into the spine. Here is the traveling that we were talking about.

Leave an area to quilt the next petal, so that it fits snuggly into the first petal.

It helps me to think of it as though the bottom of the petal "merges" into the spine. It travels along the line, but just for a short time.

The petals can touch each other, or there can be a space.

Note continues on next page

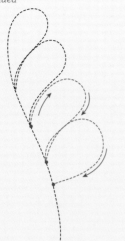  

If the petal doesn't merge into the line, it will look like this.

As you can see, it leaves no room for the next petal.

Soon your petals will be going the wrong direction.

If you notice that your petal isn't merging into the spine, travel down then start the next one. It might look weird now, but it won't be as noticeable when the quilt is finished.

This has happened to me more than once. It's more important to keep going instead of stopping.

3 Once you are finished with the first swirl, echo around the feather until you get to where you would like to add your next feather.

This doesn't have to be any certain place, just pick a spot that looks good.

4 Quilt another swirl that extends from the first one. Don't be afraid to let it go out into the unquilted area.

5 Add petals around the swirl, just as you did in the first feather.

6 Echo around the feather to get to the area you would like to quilt your next feather.

Echoing also helps you fill in any gaps between the feathers.

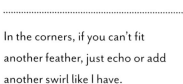

In the corners, if you can't fit another feather, just echo or add another swirl like I have.

Then, echo around until you have space to add your next one.

NOTE

You can also echo around a previously quilted feather.

Fill in gaps between feathers
with more echoing,

7 Continue quilting until the
whole area is filled.

Start

End

Other Ways to Use the Feather Meander

Quilting a single feather swirl is an easy way to fill a quilt block. It can easily fit in square or circle blocks.

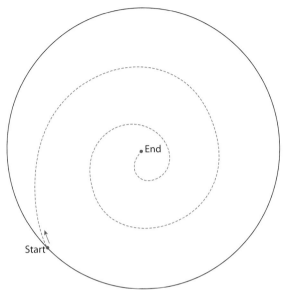

Feather in circle block, Step 1

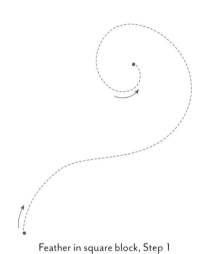

Feather in square block, Step 1

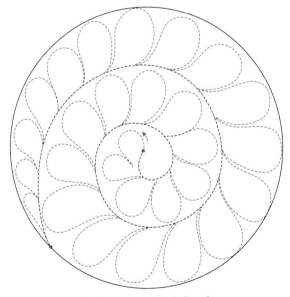

Feather in circle block, Step 2

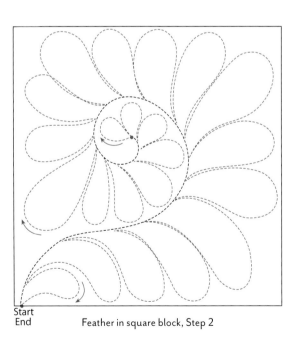

Feather in square block, Step 2

Troubleshooting FAQs ····➤

Q. Why do my petals keep going the wrong direction?

A. *Keeping the petals consistent is the probably the hardest part of this design. Practice drawing it over and over again. Once the shape becomes easy to draw, then you can try quilting it.*

Q. What side of the swirl should I add my petals on?

A. *The petals should go around the outside of the curve. If you aren't sure where to go, stop for a moment. Use your finger to trace out the next steps. It will help you see if you are headed in the right direction or not.*

Q. I followed the steps, but it doesn't look quite right. What can I do differently?

A. *The most common mistake I see with this design is quilting the petals too small. Feathers look better when they are plump and fill in the area completely. Try focusing on making the petals bigger, I promise it will look better.*

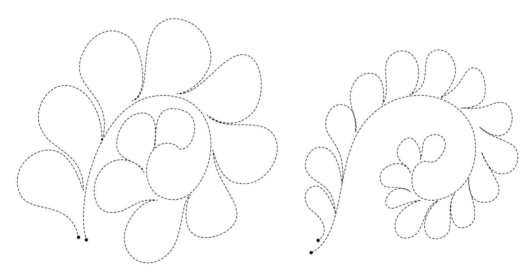

Fuller petals (*left*) tend to look better than skinnier, smaller petals (*right*).

If you have quilted your petals too skinny, just add some echoing and fill in the space.

Q. How can I improve my traveling lines, so they don't show up?

A. *Honestly, practice is the only thing that helps with traveling. But there are things you can do to make it look better. First, using a thread color that matches the quilt top will make the travel lines less noticeable. Also, if the traveling is driving you nuts, just make the petals stop short of the spine.*

It still looks good and you don't have to stress out about the lines touching each other.

IMPROV QUILTING

What you'll master:
Consistent spacing

This is the chapter when we get to bring it all together. Improv quilting allows us to combine all the designs we have learned in this book. It's a fun way to get the most use out of designs you have learned. Improv quilting keeps the quilting process interesting and adds so much interest to your quilts.

The key to improv quilting is keeping the spacing consistent. This allows the designs to blend with each other creating a nice allover texture.

Quilting the Improv Design

TIP *When I began quilting, I struggled to keep my quilting the same size throughout the quilt.* The more I quilted, the smaller my quilting would get. Keeping a drawing or a previously quilted sample close by will help give you a visual reference to use as you work your way through the quilt. ●

When combining designs, I like to divide them into "bigger" designs and "filler" designs. The "bigger" designs aren't necessarily larger they just take up a little more space than the rest. These would include:

- Paisleys ● Leaves ● Feathers

The "filler" designs are ones that don't take up as much space, making them perfect for filling in the gaps between the other quilting designs. These would include the rest of the designs in the book:

- Meander ● Loopy Meander
- Swirl Meander ● Swirl Hook Meander

1
Start by quilting one or two bigger designs, a feather and some leaves for instance.

Transitioning from one design to the next is as easy as finishing one then starting the next. If necessary, use echoing to work your way around a design until you reach the perfect area for the next one.

2
Use a "filler" design to fill in any spaces between the quilting and the edge of the area.

The meander design is perfect for this.

NOTE

If you aren't sure a design is going fit with another, take a moment and use your finger to trace it on the fabric. It will help your brain visualize where to go next.

TIP *Preventing Gaps*

I like to think of my quilting as a "blob." Keeping the quilting together helps prevent any gaps between the quilting designs. ●

Stringing out the designs may make it harder to fill the gaps later.

Keeping the quilting close together helps prevent gaps.

3 Quilt another "bigger" quilting design. How about a couple of swirls?

4 Add a few paisleys, then quilt the loopy meander to fill in between the other quilting.

5 Use the designs you want!
There is no special order or frequency you have to follow. When a design pops into mind, quilt it!

6 The corners can be a little tricky, just remember to fill them in as much as possible.

7 Have fun with it!

Hopefully by this point of the book, you are feeling more comfortable with the machine quilting process. Try to have fun with this technique. I love to let my mind wander while I quilt several fun designs.

Other Ways to Use Improv Quilting

ORGANIZED CHAOS

I like to mix up the designs because it plays right into my ADD style of machine quilting.

But, if that seems like too much bouncing around, try quilting them in sections.

Quilt a row of a "bigger" design, such as leaves.

Leave a space of a couple of inches then quilt another row of another "bigger" design, such as feathers.

It doesn't have to be perfectly spaced, or even in a perfect row.

Next, quilt the spaces in between with a "filler" design, such as the basic meander.

NOTE

If you prefer, you can just quilt the rows without leaving a space in between them. Quilt the designs in the order that works for you!

Keep repeating until the whole area is filled in.

I am quilting the swirls in this illustration.

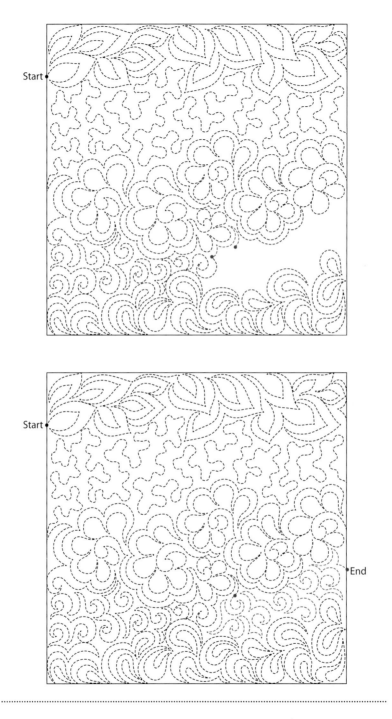

I am echoing around the feathers as well.

FOCAL POINT

Another easy way to use this technique on your quilt is to play with the scale of the quilting. Making some of the designs bigger (with more space between the lines) will make them show up more.

This is especially helpful if you want a particular design to be more prominent. For instance, let's pretend that you love quilting feathers. (I'm sure you love feathers, right? Even if you don't, you can still be friends!) Quilt them on a larger scale to show them off!

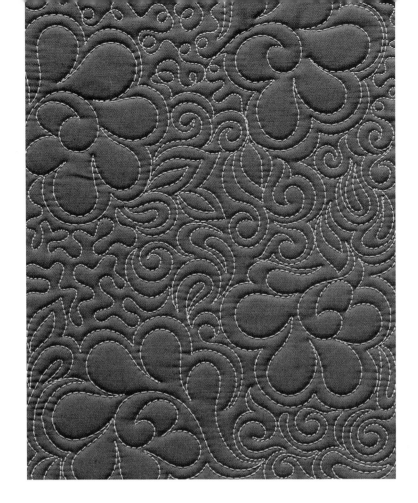

Troubleshooting FAQs ···▶

Q. How can I keep the quilting consistent?

A. *When I began quilting, I struggled to keep my quilting the same size throughout the quilt. The more I quilted, the smaller my quilting became. I quickly learned that keeping a drawing or a previously quilted sample close at hand helped me keep the spacing consistent.*

Q. How do you get the designs to "connect" without leaving a gap?

A. *It's the magical effect of echoing. Echoing helps you maneuver around an area and fills in any gaps between the designs. As long as the whole area is filled in as consistently as possible, all you will see is the overall texture of the quilting.*

YOU *ARE* READY!

Here's the deal—you can practice all you want, but nothing beats the experience that comes with quilting an actual quilt. Will it look perfect? Probably not. Will you have a finished quilt that you can actually use? Definitely.

I have said it a million times:

"A finished quilt is better than a perfect quilt top."

So now comes the point at which I release you to your quilting destiny! Happy Quilting!

ABOUT THE AUTHOR

ANGELA WALTERS is a machine quilter and author who loves to teach others to use quilting to bring out the best in their quilts. Her work has been published in numerous magazines and books. She shares tips and finished quilts on her blog, quiltingismytherapy.com, and believes that "quilting is the funnest part!"

Also by Angela Walters:

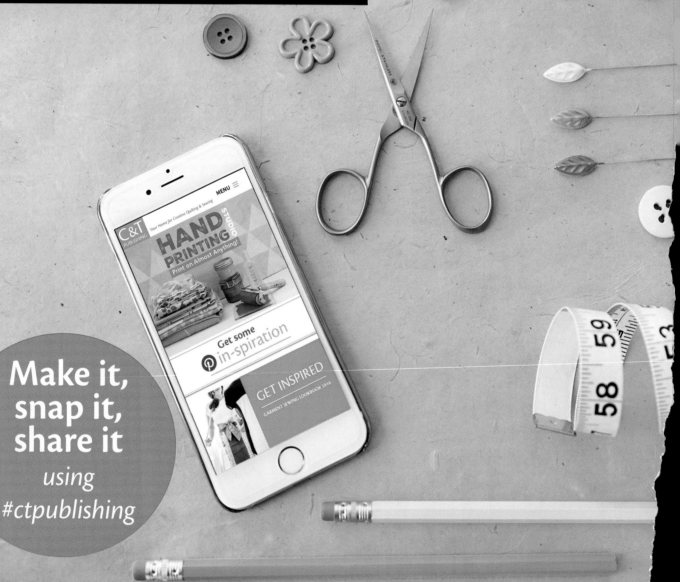